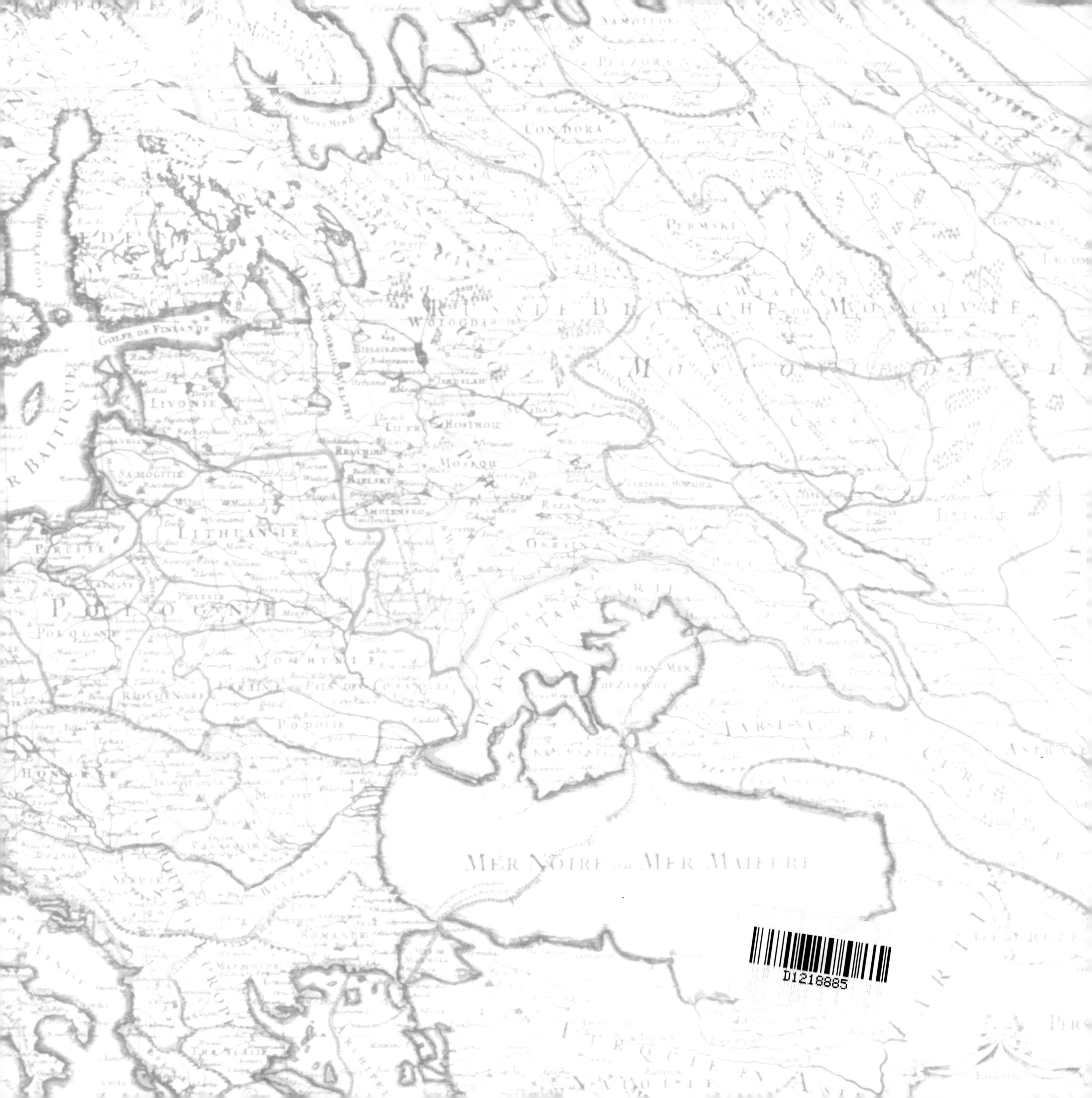
MER NOIRE ou MER MAIEURE
RUSSIE BLANCHE ou MOSCOVIE
GOLFE DE FINLANDE
MER BALTIQUE
LIVONIE
SAMOGITIE
LITHUANIE
PRUSSE
POLOGNE
VOLHYNIE
PODOLIE
HONGRIE
CONDORA
PERMSKI
WOLOGDA
ROSTHOU
MOSKOU
SMOLENSKO
RESCHOU
BIELSKI
REZAN
OKRAINA
TARTARIE
MOLDAVIE
SERVIE
ROMANIE

Pedals & Petals

greve in chianti, italy

The Fine Art Photography of
John & Debora Scanlan

IMAGES BY JOHN & DEBORA SCANLAN
TEXT BY LORI TOWNE

PUBLISHED BY
SCANLAN PORTFOLIO
52399 230th Street, Glenwood, IA 51534
712.526.2376
www.scanlan.com

For information on ordering a Scanlan limited edition photograph, visit their online gallery at www.scanlan.com or call 1.800.373.2515

First Edition

ISBN 0-9774193-0-4

Published by
Scanlan Portfolio
52399 230th Street, Glenwood, IA 51534
712.526.2376
www.scanlan.com

Text by Lori Towne
Design by Stellar Graphics
Printed in China by C&C Offset Printing Co., Ltd.
Separations by iocolor, Seattle

Dedication

we'd like to dedicate this first book and all our love

To our daughter, Haley

Acknowledgments

we would like to thank, first of all, our Lord: for the abundant blessings He daily provides, for His steady guidance, and for His constant protection as we travel. we hope to be good stewards and faithful vessels of the gifts He has given us.

we would also like to thank our parents for being the kind of role models that we can only hope to become. They have shown us enduring love, patience and support. our entire families are, to this day, a major part of our business, contributing in various but essential ways. we want them to know how much they are loved and appreciated.

we would also like to acknowledge and thank our friends for all their help and support. Many of our closest friends play important roles in our lives and in our business.

To all the above, we enthusiastically and appreciatively say, "we couldn't have done any of this without you!"

Foreword

Every time I pondered the content of this foreword, the word "perspective" kept coming to mind. What perspective should I take? From what viewpoint should I write? As a viewer, a writer, an artist, a friend? I am all of those things. I have known John and Deb Scanlan for nearly two decades, during which time our lives have continually intersected on many fronts. We began as co-workers and grew into friends, confidantes, and now, co-laborers. This book, in many ways, is a direct product of our growing relationship with each other as well as with our world. You may notice traces of that growth; indeed, that is my desire, for it is in looking back that we often obtain the best "perspective."

Over the years, I have written countless descriptions to accompany the Scanlans' images. Each and every time, the task seems daunting, if not impossible. How can I possibly do justice to an image that speaks volumes for itself? That inability, oddly enough, perhaps accounts for any mark I might eventually hit, for it forces me to do two things: first, to pray for guidance; and second, to spend time with the image.

I would encourage the first activity at all times. But I would like to suggest the second, as well. Again I recall the word "perspective." In those searching times, I find my own perspective, but so can we all — if we but take the time to explore, to see for ourselves, to experience firsthand what at first glance is only an image. Granted, these images are beautiful in and of themselves. If they were nothing more than "pretty pictures," they would serve a useful purpose. In addition, as inundated as we are with fast-moving, now-you-see-it-now-you-don't flashes of color and light, the mere pace of a still image is soothing and satisfying.

There is much more to a Scanlan photograph, however. Underlying each image are nuances of meaning that only come to light when time is taken to consider them. The "story" that emerges may vary from person to person, but a difference in perspectives, rather than invalidating the "real" story, only enhances the image's worth. The exploration of the image is part and parcel of its value.

The Scanlans naturally approach the scenes they photograph with their own, unique perspective. They see with an artist's eye; they notice balance and rhythm, harmony, color, light, drama. They even seek them out. But herein lies a viewpoint that differs from much of the rest of the world: they take no credit for what they find. They merely count themselves lucky — or, more accurately, blessed — by what they have been allowed to see, and more important, to share. They are not out for "effect." They are not out for "success" by others' standards. They judge themselves successful if their images touch someone in some small but meaningful way.

I am one of those blessed to be greatly touched by Scanlan images. They would humbly, incredulously disavow that their work is capable of such a thing. But I can assure you that it is. By the time I finish writing about my journey into an image, I feel ownership in it. It has become part of me, in my experience of it. It is this same exploration that I would urge you to undertake. I promise you, the effort to find your own perspective will not be in vain.

— Lori Towne

Sunlit Gondolier

When light and water play, the game is delightful to watch. And in a city like Venice, water itself can become the playing field.

In a watery Venetian "street" already lit with soft, inviting hues, we noticed light streaming down the canal, shimmering on the water's surface. We set up our cameras and waited for all the players to join in.

Moments passed, travelers passed. Then, in a flash, a gondolier passed. The light caught a long oar perfectly, then sent its glowing reflection to the waiting water, which, ever cooperative, passed it down the canal to us.

venice, italy

St. Finbar's Retreat

catching a glimpse of the reclusive st. finbar was probably as tentative as catching a shot of the chapel in his haunting grounds in gougane barra national park in county cork.

for the moment only, the water near that little chapel was still, the sky above it was clear, and the rhododendrons engulfing it were fragrant. we moved quickly in the moment and the season, keenly aware that the disruptive wind was moving in and the delicate spring was moving out.

county cork, ireland

Rocky Cathedrals

We were on our way to Venice through the Dolomite mountains in northern Italy, when we decided to avail ourselves of the rare break in the gloomy weather and head north to a village about a hundred miles outside our planned route. At the end of a box canyon, the village sits quietly — secretly almost, for the mountains give no portent of the scene they conceal. Coming upon it, we were awestruck. The only sounds in this grand place came from church bells ringing in the distance, the stream rushing below us, the cow bells clinking in the hills.

We quickly set up our camera, racing against the fickle light. Twenty minutes later, the scene — with its divinely granted light and color and shadow — was gone: the sun dropped below the mountains behind us, the clouds shrouded the peaks, and the village receded in the dusky darkness, hidden once again.

Dolomites, Italy

A Resting Place

where better to rest one's heart than in the heart of ireland?

After enjoying a mellow sunday dinner in an irish pub, we decided to take an evening drive. in the heart of connemara, near clifden, we paused — for the surroundings seemed to do the same. Resting in the shadows of the 12 pins mountains, pine and pond came together to offer a bit of space and a bit of peace.

connemara, ireland

The Journey

How long is our journey, compared to the history of the world?

It may seem insignificant, measured against the enormity of the earth. Or it may seem short, compared with tangible signs of the earth's age.

Near a winery in Chianti, one man walked out his immediate destiny, undaunted by his diminutive relationship with the measuring rod of ancient cypress trees that flanked his path.

Tuscany, Italy

Eilean Donan

The definitive scottish castle in the definitive scottish atmosphere: that is Eilean Donan castle in the morning.

Located on the Isle of skye, the renowned, ancient castle has appeared in many modern films, long outlasting its now-obscure inhabitants. we took a shot of the castle one evening, when both the tide and the sun were out. somehow, it seemed "too nice."

so we came back in the morning. The tide was in and the sun was hiding. Mist clung to the hills, tinging both the vegetation and the atmosphere. water covered the rock and earth surrounding the castle, conjuring up a glassy reflection. seeing now with our eyes what we had seen in our mind's eye, it seemed that time had been turned back centuries in the span of just a few hours.

The Highlands, Scotland

Rising Light

Morning. when the light is gentle and the world seems new.

After a day of being buffeted by wind, the island of santorini woke up to a quiet october sky. The restlessness of the previous day had been swept into the air, leaving the only remnant of its violence in a display of gentle hues. Dust raised by the wind and gathered into the atmosphere spread an orange glow from horizon to horizon, and an even, fresh light from rooftop to rooftop.

oia, greece

A Day's Repose

Everything on the Greek Isle of Santorini seems designed for one time of day — sunset.

White-washed buildings, blue domes, bell towers all expectantly stand watch over the sea. Human spectators gather every evening as the sun meets the waters, and clap in homage to the show's creator.

Desiring a private viewing, we returned to the island in April, a month noted for storms that drive skies into a frenzy and visitors into refuge. After three days of heavy winds, the sky churned like a boiling stew. Then, as the winds calmed, so did the waters. And all that watched — both human and inanimate — saw the brilliant reward of reaching another day's close.

santorini, greece

Alpine Church

Nature's whims can defy outdoor photography.

For the seventh consecutive day, we awoke in the village of Ramsau to some variety of foul weather that foiled our plans to get a shot of a church nestled in an alpine hillside.

This morning, it was fog. Ready to surrender, we were instead encouraged to drive 800 meters higher. Along the highest road in Germany, the sun suddenly popped out; we could see the tips of the Alps! The fog was rising!

We hurried back, just in time to witness nature's unveiling of the church in the valley, as we before had only imaged.

Bavarian Alps, Germany

Embracing the Night

As we travel, we become aware that the laws of the natural world apply universally. The simple consistency in the rising and the setting of the sun reminds us of our commonalities, rather than our differences. The sun rests at the end of the day in the outer reaches of our world, just as it does at home. Even so, the sun's recline can stand out as unusual in any locale. Sitting outside in the rooftop restaurant of a Prague hotel, we witnessed one of those sunsets that etch themselves into memory. As we enjoyed our meal in the evening air, warm despite the day's drawing closed, the lights in the old town square illuminated shadowy forms, like ghosts of the past. Above, the sky slowly transformed itself under the sun's sleepy eye. Like a rose blooming, pale pink became scarlet, then lavender, then violet. And we sat, amazed, again, at the wonder of the world, that its beauty can find us wherever we are.

prague, czech republic

Reflections of Prague

Just outside Prague, and just after nightfall, we found yet another image that spoke to the city's history and perhaps its very essence. In the depths of the dark sky and river, Prague glowed golden. The town castle, neighboring churches, and nearby buildings illuminated the night air and reflected off the moving water. Every detail became apparent, as we opened our lens and waited. And once again, we were struck by the recurring theme sustained visually and metaphorically by the new Czech Republic: light — hopeful and unremitting — shining in the dark.

Charles Bridge

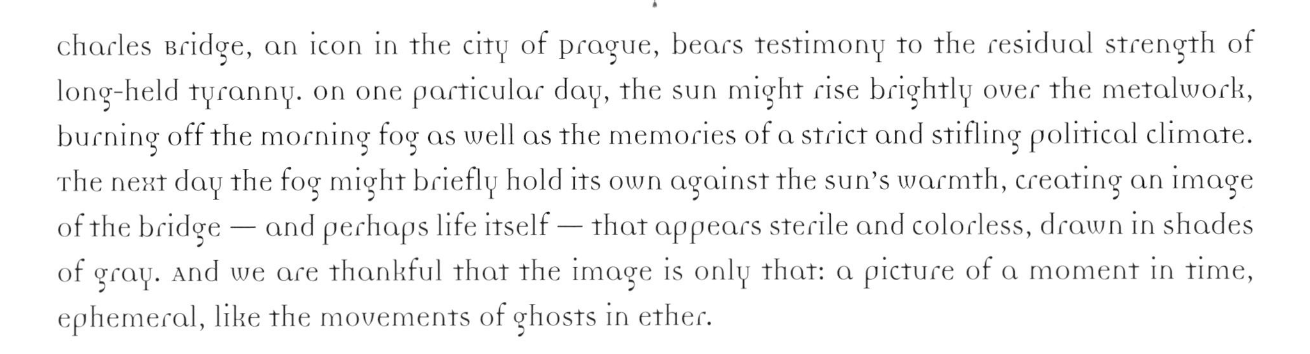

Charles Bridge, an icon in the city of Prague, bears testimony to the residual strength of long-held tyranny. On one particular day, the sun might rise brightly over the metalwork, burning off the morning fog as well as the memories of a strict and stifling political climate. The next day the fog might briefly hold its own against the sun's warmth, creating an image of the bridge — and perhaps life itself — that appears sterile and colorless, drawn in shades of gray. And we are thankful that the image is only that: a picture of a moment in time, ephemeral, like the movements of ghosts in ether.

prague, czech republic

Caldera

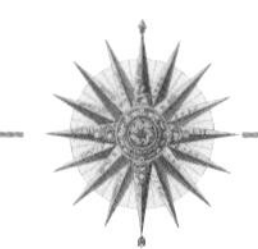

Life on Santorini, Greece, ironically owes its existence to a destructive force.

The island was formed by volcanic activity, of the kind that collapsed a volcano in 1650 B.C. and left a "caldera" in its place. When water filled the caldera, a lake was born — and evidence of its maker was obscured.

Still, reminders of the now-submerged volcano abound. Rock is piled upon rock, just as homes are built upon homes, climbing up the cliff sides. Vineyards spring from the fertile soil that was once lava and ash. Fishermen plumb the caldera's depths for the catch of the day at local eateries, many of which they also own.

But in the day-to-day activity of life, it may be easy to forget the peril that once destroyed and may yet threaten — especially when the view from most any window is breathtaking.

santorini, greece

Swan Lake

It took us eight years to get back to Hallstatt, Austria, and one day to get the shot we wanted. When we saw "Swan Lake" in 1991, we realized its potential. We also knew that capturing the drama of this classic scene would call for a unique lighting situation. The day we arrived, it was calm, but disappointingly foggy. We went anyway, just to check out the general layout of the scene. As we got closer, the fog started to lift, quite rapidly. By the time we set up, the sun lit the fog in the distance, the water shimmered with smooth reflections, and the town itself seemed both to float on the water and to hover in the sky — all on a surprising first day.

Lake Hallstattersee, Hallstatt, Austria

Fallen Petals

In an ancient town in ancient mountains where timelessness pervades the new as readily as the old, even the flowers seem to know their place in the world, their place in the march. we were as content as the flower petals, to stop and rest on these chairs, in their village, near their castle, high atop their hill, in their quiet valley, surrounded by their foothills, by their mountains. our shutter paused to close — it too, taking its time, in four long seconds carefully drawing from the warm sky its glow and from the errant petals, the memories.

gruyeres, switzerland

Life is but a Dream

On a balmy summer afternoon in the old Portuguese seaside town of Nazarre, a fishing boat sat lonely on the beach as a testament to the pursuit that has sustained this area for centuries. Larger than it seems, the boat measures more than six feet high at the bow, making it quite immense for a "row boat."

nazare, portugal

Scattered Blossoms

The same sun that shines on the rest of the world shines on Bellagio, Italy, on the shores of Lake Como. But could it be that it has a special fondness for this town? In a pretty little spot in an outdoor café, the sun found, as we did, a growth of wisteria it could not leave alone. Gentle rays seemed to caress the wisteria's abundant blooms, brushing off violet petals here and there, and sprinkling them like cool rain onto the tables and chairs waiting, like diners, for refreshment.

Lake Como, Italy

Mykonos

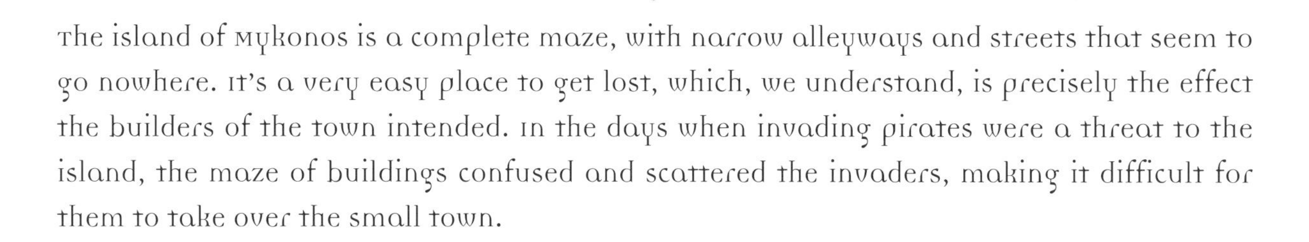

The island of Mykonos is a complete maze, with narrow alleyways and streets that seem to go nowhere. It's a very easy place to get lost, which, we understand, is precisely the effect the builders of the town intended. In the days when invading pirates were a threat to the island, the maze of buildings confused and scattered the invaders, making it difficult for them to take over the small town.

Mykonos, Greece

Nordic Harbour

Fishing is one of Norway's largest industries, it's only natural that we encountered a number of tiny fishing villages. Featured here is the very unique village of Hamnoy, located in the Lofoten Islands. It seems strange to refer to fishing as an "industry," but it is an enterprise that keeps these people going. They make the best of what they have and what they have a lot of is access to the sea! It was a bright, beautiful day and I was thrilled to capture this close up view of the village with the wispy sky in the background. "Nordic Harbour" is an invitation to another world rich with tradition and pride in a hearty heritage.

Hamnoy, Norway

Awakening

In the dark, you have two choices: stay in bed, or go look for the sunrise.

For three days, I had hoped for a memorable shot of Venice's Grand Canal, where the church of Salute rises majestically. For three days, perpetual rain washed away those hopes. Staying in bed seemed a viable option for Day 4.

Nevertheless, dawn found me making my way through dark alleyways to the Academia Bridge. Clouds hovered on the horizon, giving no indication of their intentions. I confess to thinking, "This could be bad, or this could be fantastic."

Suffice it to say, I am glad that Day 4 didn't awake without me.

venice, italy

A Walk to Remember

The journey and the destination — both seem like the same surreal dream in Villa Cimbrone, in Ravello, Italy. Walking through wisteria vines dangling over a seemingly endless pathway, you are engulfed and intoxicated by the heavy scent of spring. When the pathway does finally end, you find yourself at the "bluest view in the world." As if dreaming, you feel yourself overtaken by the sense that the world is not as you had expected — that once separate sky and ocean have now somehow merged. And all is only blue.

Ravello, Italy

Vernazza

we can go to great lengths to get to great heights. The hike to a lofty spot in Vernazza, one of the five Cinque Terre villages in Italy, was temporarily challenging but ultimately rewarding. After climbing with a backpack loaded with photography equipment, we found the bird's-eye view from this vantage point as visually intense as the ascent had been physically intense. We felt part of the scene itself, perched on the hillside like the buildings around us, peering over the water like the windows across the cove, and basking like the entire village in the warmth of the day's last rays of light.

cinque terre, italy

Old Course

For four centuries, golf has been played on the Old Course at St. Andrews. For just as long, perhaps, golfers have dreamed of journeying to this veritable golfing wellspring.

The course is not alone in luring visitors: the Links Clubhouse, the Old Course Hotel, and the Royal and Ancient Golf Club are attractions in their own right.

But perhaps most recognizable is a manmade feature on the last hole: the Swilcan Bridge, named for the Swilcan Burn, a stream that wanders across the first and 18th fairways. Originally designed for routine access from town to harbor rather than golfing convenience, the stone bridge has nonetheless become inextricably identified with the course — an icon of an icon.

st. Andrews, scotland

Corner Stones

In a fortified village atop a hill near the French Riviera, an endless maze of alleyways led us to a quiet corner. In the corner, we found a pile of stones as carefully arranged as the exquisite homes that adorned the nearby hills and as gentle and warm as the Mediterranean landscape itself.

provence, france

Provence in Bloom

purple: A royal color with rural roots.

By another name, it is lavender, whose history is richly defined by kings and servants alike. charles VI of France is said to have demanded lavender-filled pillows wherever he went, perhaps inspired — or spoiled — by the fragrant blooms growing profusely in the French region of provence.

prized for its herbal, medicinal, aromatic and romantic use, lavender has ancient roots. Legend holds that Mary dried Jesus' swaddling clothes on a lavender bush, a tradition maintained by laundry maids whose practice earned them the name "lavenders." It was lavender — "a pound of ointment of spikenard" — that was used to anoint Jesus' feet, and whose fragrance filled the house.

surely such an effect is familiar to rural provence residents blessed enough to make their home near the royal fields of purple.

provence, france

Rue-du-Fleuri

There is a village in Alsace we cannot seem to stay away from, or get enough of. No matter how many times we go back, we find something new. It is a village where the smell of wine — of grapes being pressed — hangs in the air; where grape juice runs through the crevices of the cobblestone paths that lead from one enchanting alleyway to another. We invariably find ourselves drawn about the village, as if entranced by each new discovery on these purplish paths. On one such street, we paused. Flowers and foliage spilled over balconies, painted walls alternately cooled and warmed the passageway. For several days, we returned to this "Rue du Fleuri," this street of flowers, watching the light play, until we knew that the camera could capture what we had already seen with our hearts.

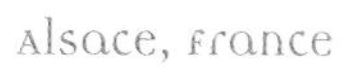

Alsace, France

Floral Ascent

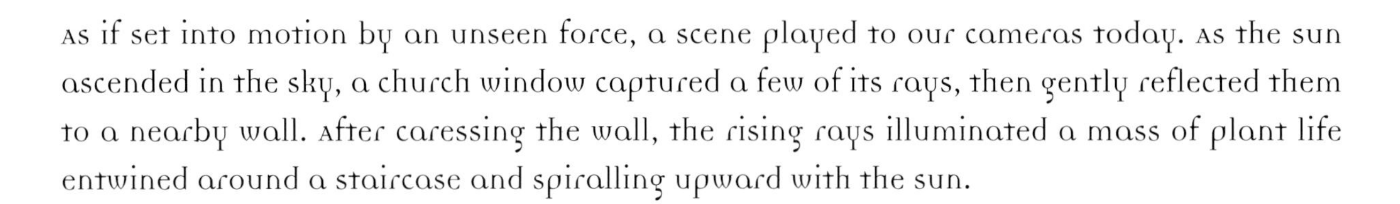

As if set into motion by an unseen force, a scene played to our cameras today. As the sun ascended in the sky, a church window captured a few of its rays, then gently reflected them to a nearby wall. After caressing the wall, the rising rays illuminated a mass of plant life entwined around a staircase and spiralling upward with the sun.

Alsace, France

Time in a Bottle

Ideas and wine: Two things that get better with age.

The longer one believes something, the more the idea seems valid. Wine-makers definitely had the right idea when they decided to bottle their creations — and to make wine in the first place. But it is said that grapes begin to ferment within seven seconds of being crushed, so man may have had little more to do than contain the exquisite process. In that, wine-making is somewhat like photography, which captures the processes of life — but is even more like ideas, which, once postulated, take on a life of their own.

Tuscany, Italy

Bon Appétit

Warmth clings to the town of Sarlat, France, as tenaciously as its buildings cling to cliffs and hillsides.

The auburn stone indigenous to the area exudes warmth from the town's walls even on the coolest, wettest days. Walking through an alleyway in weather that had chased most inside, we saw a scene that invited outdoor dalliance in spite of the alternating mist and rain. Tables, chairs, flowers — and a backdrop of that honey-colored stone — were all we needed for our invitation to sit, rest, and sip.

sarlat, france

Roman Numerals

what's in a number?

plenty, in some cases. Although Arabic numerals were known to the western world by 1000 A.D. or before, Europe resisted their use, even banning them in various places in favor of Roman numerals. So it is no surprise that even in 1607, a builder in Alsace, France, was still using the ancient Roman system.

what does surprise is that buildings from that era still stand. 400 years later, they remain in such good structural condition that many simply receive fresh stucco and new windows or doors. And perhaps a new house number.

Ribeauville, France

Steps in Time

The scene may have been vacant when we found it, but our steps were not the first taken there. In a village tucked into the hills of the Alsace region of France, a stone staircase climbed a wall. A short distance away, a small church stood. Beyond the church, rows and rows of vineyards lined the hillsides. Storks nested atop the town's various churches and in the higher-steepled homes. Quiet yet busy, in its own way. That much, we could surmise by looking at the stairs leading upward, or at the threshold across the street. The doors were silent as to use, as they no doubt had been replaced over the centuries. But the stone, holding fast without the benefit of a face lift, told a story of age and activity. Worn away to curving lines the stone must have endured thousands — perhaps millions — of footsteps of residents and visitors, once here and now gone.

Alsace, France

Vintage Fox

A fox hidden among leaves isn't a strange sight. But one holding a wine bottle in front of a French restaurant?

Actually, it makes an odd kind of sense, when you consider a few facts about the fox. His diet includes fruits and berries, he has an acute sense of smell, and he adapts to a wide range of habitats — even a French street. Moreover, his life span is similar to that of a good wine, three to six years for him, five to seven for the wine.

On our initial visit, we couldn't determine the exact "vintage" of the fox. On a return trip, however, the absence of our preserved friend suggested that he — like many a fermented beverage — had passed his prime.

Riquewihr, France

Brushstrokes

One wonders if Monet painted his garden as he saw it, or if he planted his garden according to his impression of the world.

In the spring, Monet's garden looks like his paintings themselves, as tulips, iris, hyacinths and sundry foliage explode in color. The garden is bathed in subtle hues, nearly indescript as splashes of violet, red, yellow and green wash over one another.

Did Monet see all of life as it grew in his garden, or lacking that, did he purposely cultivate his vision where he could? It's a question not restricted just to the realm of paint and canvas, but which extends appropriately to the dominion of lens and emulsion as well.

giverny, france

Poulbot

Like an oft-told fairy tale. Like spritely characters reborn from childhood memory as faint, ghostly outlines. Like fancy and whimsy and delight. Like Paris. High on the only hilltop in Paris, the artist colony of Montmartre hides a quiet restaurant named "Poulbot." The front window, itself covered with fanciful figures from some unknown fantasy, frames another scene — illustrates another tale — playing out inside the tiny café. Under the glow of soft light, patrons speak in low tones, telling their stories on a gentle stage set with lace curtains gracing a wooden door, antique pitchers suspended by hooks, and prized photographs dimly illuminated. Outside the window on the day we found Poulbot, the air was cold, the sky was threatening. But, somehow, everything seemed all right. The light was right. The colors were right. The story was right.

paris, france

Les fleurs a Suzette

when the larger world seems overwhelmed by destruction, small corners of the world nevertheless rigorously profess life.

shortly after 9/11, we visited France, a country once torn by the strife of war. we encountered a woman whose heart likely still held those memories. while asking to photograph her house, we identified ourselves as Americans. Immediately, tears filled her eyes, and she managed the one word we could understand: "catastrophe."

A world away, yet she felt kinship with those suffering in another. As we looked at her tiny yard, overflowing with abundant life, we could not say it had always been so. But we were certain that at least one corner of the world, in this place or another, would forever assert a defiant testimony to prevailing life in the face of the powers that would destroy.

Loire Valley, France

Monet's Inspiration

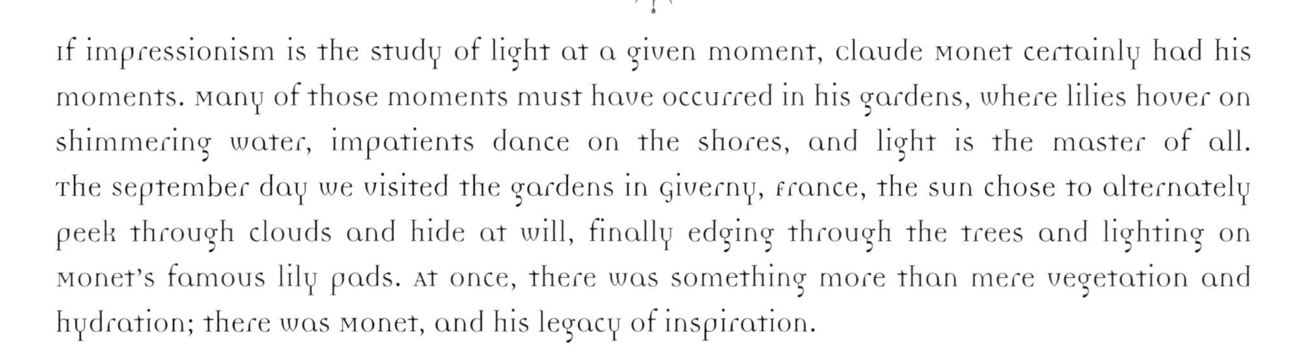

If impressionism is the study of light at a given moment, Claude Monet certainly had his moments. Many of those moments must have occurred in his gardens, where lilies hover on shimmering water, impatients dance on the shores, and light is the master of all. The September day we visited the gardens in Giverny, France, the sun chose to alternately peek through clouds and hide at will, finally edging through the trees and lighting on Monet's famous lily pads. At once, there was something more than mere vegetation and hydration; there was Monet, and his legacy of inspiration.

Giverny, France

Menu of the Day

Part of the appetite for life lies in its colors. The French must know this — and they are known for their appetite for life. In Honfleur, France, on the Normandy coast, a small café sits at the end of the harbor. The patrons of this little place don't come merely for the food, however, but for all of what their eyes can feast upon. The activity in the harbor captures their attention, most certainly, yet there is more. The blues and yellows of the café, bright and luscious on their own, are made yet more delicious in tandem. And the partakers of this tableaux are filled to the brim with a uniquely satisfying banquet of visuals and victuals.

Honfleur, France

Veiled Garden

we had experienced the beauty of stourhead gardens, in the county of wiltshire, England. we knew to expect rich foliage and ancient, towering timbers surrounding a glistening lake. we had seen the Roman columns artistically erected here and there, the little church that stood near the lake. what we could not predict, however, was how Nature would bring a few important elements together the morning we woke to fog lifting over the lake. Down at the water's edge, azaleas and rhododendrons were blooming in the glory of late spring. The water lay motionless, its surface undisturbed and placid in the early-morning calm. A faint mist, the remnants of the lifting fog, was pierced here and there by the warming sun. Glowing with gentle light, the mist clung tenaciously to an arching foot bridge, as if it were as reluctant to depart as we were.

wiltshire, England

La Maison Antoinette

It may well be said that Marie Antoinette lived in her own little world.

Whatever the accuracy of that figurative statement, there is at least one realm where those words are literally true. On the outskirts of the royal Versailles estate, small cottages circle a lake. While not surprising in themselves, these cottages take on a different shape when their history is revealed. Marie had these homes built as part of a hamlet — a miniature village — for herself. They became, in essence, here own personal "doll house" village, through which she could stroll and, it is said, feel more like a commoner and less like royalty.

versailles, france

Marie's Hamlet

One gets tired of being a queen, we suppose — or perhaps of acting like one.

Marie Antoinette's regal position afforded her the opportunity to create her own little world, where she could "play" at being common. On the grounds of Versailles, Marie had built a village of "dollhouses" that seems at once fair-tale like and quite French. Brick cottages poke up among pumpkins and asters, stone pathways meander among grass and trees.

In the village inspired by imagination, one can easily imagine Marie looking out through a tiny cottage window, not at her grand court, but at her simple courtyard.

versailles, france

Cottage Thatch

Although we didn't know it until afterwards, timing was critical for one of our shots today. Shortly after photographing a thatched-roof cottage, one of a block of interconnected homes, a woman appeared from within the house. Moments later, she rode off on the bicycle parked in front, taking it out of the shot!

county Limerick, Ireland

Dusk

After trudging through ankle-deep mud and dodging a horse interested in making a snack of us, we settled down to wait for the light to work its magic in the dusk. Although we took the same shot last night, the warmth of the light today (John's birthday!) created a glow on the ancient rock of an abandoned castle near the coast of County Galway.

connemara, ireland

Celtic Passage

Along a coastal road that skirts the burren, a mountainous region almost entirely covered with rocks, we found a graveyard built on one of the few spots of bare earth in the area. curious to see if any of our ancestors had found a permanent home there, we wandered through the green grass, scanning the names on the ancient markers. sure enough, we discovered what we were looking for in this moody, ethereal place.

county clare, ireland

A Soft Day

A hard shot on a soft day. What made a scene perfect made it perfectly difficult to get. We discovered a setting with all the components of the Irish landscape paradigm: sheep lounging in a gully, a stone bridge spanning a meandering stream, lush grass clinging to a craggy landscape, mist hanging in the background. But on this day on the isle, other elements were at work. We cooperated. Our tripod hugged the ground to escape the wind, and our camera took refuge under an umbrella to escape the mist on this "soft" day.

county kerry, ireland

Sea of Blue

The town of Kinsale loves color — the brighter, the better. Perhaps the sentiment formed in reaction to the subtlety of Ireland's atmosphere; skies are overcast about half the time all year long.

As we walked through Kinsale one afternoon, we came across some interesting symbolism in the vivid sapphire "waves" of a rough stucco wall. A brilliant yellow window box and frame appeared to resemble Ireland itself — spilling over with green, and floating in a sea of blue.

county cork, ireland

O'Shea's

Just in case visitors to County Kerry, Ireland, forget where they are, O'Shea's pub will remind them.

Located in a spot that seems to be on the way to everything, the Irish pub can't be missed. Other things also can't be missed: the dozens of old Irish mugs in the front window — in case one wonders about the pub's longevity; the picture of folks drinking an Irish Guinness — in case one wonders about its fare; the sign touting "Traditional Irish Music" — in case one wonders about its musical offerings; and the name of the place itself, "Kerry's Vintage Inn" — in case one wonders about its ethnic authenticity.

County Kerry, Ireland

Cambray's Farmhouse

A range of hills in southwest England, the Cotswold Hills, are noted for their uniquely colored stone. We found evidence of the stone's colorful presence in "Cambray's Farmhouse," a home offset beautifully by its proud owner's cottage garden out front (not to mention the rock garden and pond out back, of which he was equally proud!).

cotswolds, england

Castle Combe

After trying to capture castle combe on film yesterday, and being frustrated by unrelenting interruptions through the midst of the scene, we succeeded in creating an image of the manor house today. It seems most of wiltshire's inhabitants were off enjoying a morning at the races, making for a much calmer, more typical scene around the house. That's the way we will always remember it and, undoubtedly, the way it will remain for years to come, as the town itself has been placed in national trust.

wiltshire, england

Gold Hill

Shaftesbury sits like a golden jewel in the heart of Dorset, England.

The rural market town was founded among lush, rolling hills by King Alfred the Great in the 9th century. Alfred, acclaimed as one of the best kings in history, is noted for supporting religion, scholarship and education, and for defending against foreign trespass and domestic lawlessness.

On a steep road careening down the 700-foot bluff that Shaftesbury calls home, testaments to Alfred's influence yet remain. The heraldic St. Peter's church stands at the top of the cobbled street and the protective Gold Hill wall runs its length. And, as if recalling Alfred's military in miniature, cottages closed in rank like toy soldiers seem to keep one another from toppling down the golden hill into neighboring Blackmore Vale.

Dorset, England

Rose Cottage

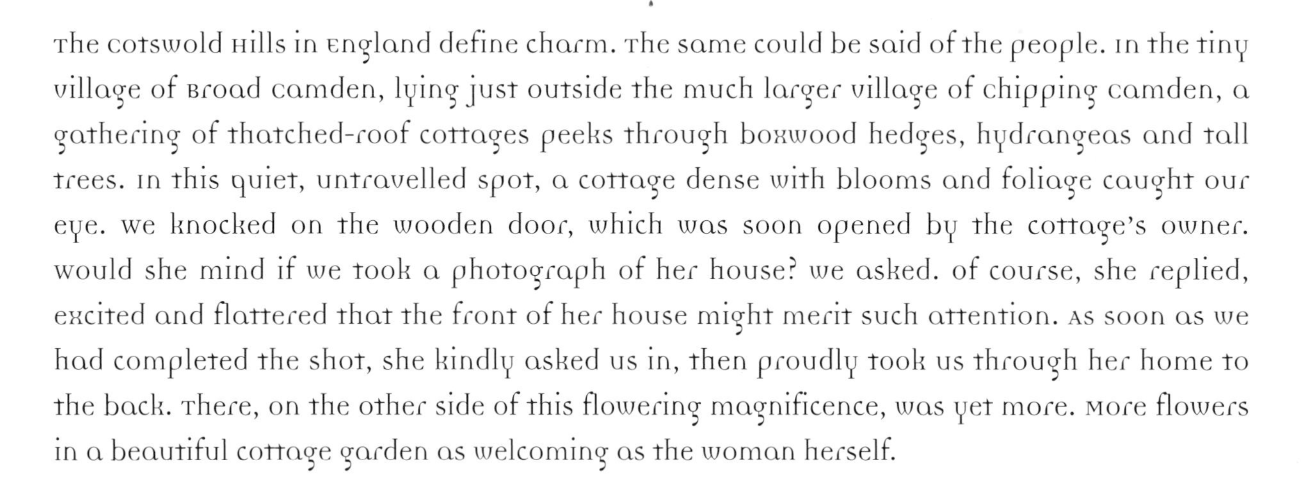

The Cotswold Hills in England define charm. The same could be said of the people. In the tiny village of Broad Camden, lying just outside the much larger village of Chipping Camden, a gathering of thatched-roof cottages peeks through boxwood hedges, hydrangeas and tall trees. In this quiet, untravelled spot, a cottage dense with blooms and foliage caught our eye. We knocked on the wooden door, which was soon opened by the cottage's owner. Would she mind if we took a photograph of her house? we asked. Of course, she replied, excited and flattered that the front of her house might merit such attention. As soon as we had completed the shot, she kindly asked us in, then proudly took us through her home to the back. There, on the other side of this flowering magnificence, was yet more. More flowers in a beautiful cottage garden as welcoming as the woman herself.

cotswolds, England

Tranquil Reflections

We had previously experienced the beauty of Stourhead Gardens, in the county of Wiltshire, England. We knew to expect rich foliage and ancient, towering timbers surrounding a glistening lake. We had seen the Roman columns artistically erected here and there, the little church that stood near the lake.

What we could not predict, however, was how nature would bring a few important elements together the morning we woke to fog lifting over the lake.

Down at the water's edge, azaleas and rhododendrons were blooming in the glory of late spring. The water lay motionless, its surface undisturbed and placid in the early-morning calm. A faint mist, the remnants of the lifting fog, was pierced here and there by the warming sun. Glowing with gentle light, the mist clung tenaciously to an arching foot bridge, as if it were as reluctant to depart as we were.

wiltshire, england

Castle Gardens

Hadden Hall, considered one of the most romantic English manor homes, is noted for its spectacular roses. The gardener put us in contact with a gentleman who gave us permission to bring our equipment into the gardens. We were given a special tour and access to all the estate grounds. Nestled on the side of a hill above a lazy river, Hadden Hall is the epitome of romance. It's clearly evident that tremendous care has been taken to maintain the grounds and gardens.

Derbyshire, England

Gatekeeper

The ruler of all he surveys. That was the impression we got from the leonine fixture outside a cottage in the gentle Cotswold Hills. Although a plaque nearby read, "Mary's Cottage," we had the feeling this was a shared domain, or at least one whose borders were warily regarded if not stringently enforced.

cotswolds, england

Bicycle

perhaps calmness belies chaos, or at least hides it!

while in cambridge, surrounded by buildings owing their design to gothic architecture, a doorway fascinated us. It was an altogether typical doorway, one you might see at any of the entrances to the several colleges of cambridge.

This particular doorway, which led to Trinity college, seemed calm yet intriguing at every level. A stilled bicycle, an opened door, a distant doorway beckoning visitors to cross the threshold.

And the reality? Not a singular bicycle, but hundreds just inside the doorway. And not a solitary bicycle, but well companied by the dozens of people who passed through this busy pedestrian street. we seized upon that fleeting moment of stillness — and will remember to remind ourselves that we may choose to find peace where we will.

cambridge, england

Cucciolo

A unique, colorful door caught our attention as we were making our way through Bordighera, on the Italian Riviera. The colors, texture and design of the door were fascinating, so we stopped and set up. After taking a couple shots, a dog jumped up from the other side of the door, stretched out his legs, crossing them, then settled in as if he would be content to hang out for hours that way while we took his photograph. We complied, enjoying the unsolicited but friendly addition to the scene.

Bordighera, Italy

First Mate

On the Italian Riviera, it seems as if almost everyone owns or operates a boat — even a cat. While he may have just been looking for a sunny spot to perch himself, or for fish scraps left behind by his owner, the cat we found in an idle boat looked as if he could easily command it. Intrigued by the clicking sounds we made, this lively pussy cat happily stayed put for several shots in his colorful boat, even squinting against the sun to remain a photographic subject.

portofino, italy

Wash Day

water for a road, mosaic slate for a walkway, purple stucco for a wall, wind for a dryer.

could wash days in Burano, Italy, and anywhere in America be more different?

The island outside venice is a photographer's dream. The bright, busy colors so familiar to the residents invariably strike visitors as spectacular, even in their unassuming environs. It is this simple beauty that holds one's attention, where even laundry hanging outdoors somehow seems intuitively, unpretentiously, perfectly placed.

Burano, Italy

Burano

A canal is at once busy and peaceful. The stillness of docked boats belies the activity that often precedes it, in this case, the "cruising" of the canals — in boats — by Italian teenagers. Teens must be the same the world over; the type of vehicle may just vary! (And perhaps their choice of beverage?)

Burano, Italy

Table for Two

About halfway between Rialto Bridge and San Marco Square, two bustling spots in a busy city, lies a canal that looks as if it could be home to romantic traffic as well as the customary water traffic. When we saw a table set for two, overlooking passing boats and gondolas, we pictured ourselves resting in that place, perhaps sipping an espresso. Although the boat traffic and the low lighting conditions (and the imminent rain) posed photographic challenges, we were sure romance was worth the effort.

venice, italy

Three Pear

some walls cry out to be painted — but not in the usual homeowners' sense.

In Burano, Italy, a stucco wall seemed almost better suited as a canvas. Red-orange impasto covered the support. White strokes lined an inner frame. Green swaths formed a vertical pattern. And the final touch: three pears sat front and center, as if hand-placed by the artist himself.

Merely a window in a wall? Or an outdoor still life?

Burano, Italy

Orvieto

The heart of Orvieto, Italy, holds an assortment of unexpected treasures, like the unassuming little shop run by a local toy-maker. He had lined his outer walls with delicate trees, one apparently a bit more delicate than the others. This lone tree had succumbed to the "other side," leaving its pristine silhouette softly etched upon a wash of warm color on the wall behind it. The quiet simplicity held me and I knew I had to get the shot. Interrupting the perfection was, of all things, a car. Refusing to be deterred I went back to the scene throughout the day, again, and again, without luck; the car remained. One last time I returned. As I approached the scene, I saw something that had not been there before as well as something missing. A glowing, dusky light, certainly not possible until this very time of day, was filling the little alleyway; and the obstructing car was gone.

umbria, italy

Sangiovese

some get to be leaves, some get to be grapes.

of course, in the chianti region of italy, it's understandable that one would want to be a grape, especially a sangiovese, for this grape is destined for inclusion in most wines from this area. in fact, chianti wine is not chianti wine without the sangiovese. if that weren't reason enough for pride, the fruit's rich color and abundant growth could make its neighbors green with envy, or even multi-hued, at the end of a long season.

chianti, italy

Café Arcade

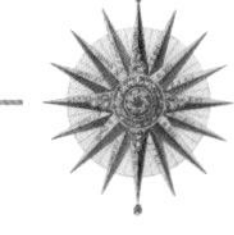

On the way to what would become Venetian Dance, we saw something we'd seen many times before, but differently. Given the early hour (6 a.m.), the café we had passed a dozen times suddenly took on a new light.

The café sits just off St. Mark's Square, near Doges Palace and next to St. Mark's Basilica, in an arcade that houses jewelry stores, shops and restaurants. This popular café, typically bustling, and its tables, almost always occupied, were empty and quiet. Now what spoke were simply the smooth lines of the darkly framed chairs; the subdued, shining tiles; the softly colored tablecloths; the rough pillars — all taking their respective places in a march of gently receding lines.

venice, italy

Venetian Dance

one April in venice, as we looked out across the water from st. Mark's square to the island of st. georgio, the actual shot took what seemed like an eternity: a minute and a half with the shutter open. we staked out the shot at 6 a.m. with the brightly lit st. georgio sitting calmly in the background, the water in front of us surged up and down, juggling the gondolas and splashing up over their sides. As it turned out "time" did indeed come through. In that long minute and a half, the shutter had taken it all in, etching the motion onto film. what we saw before us now on photographic paper seemed like the ephemeral ghosts of times past merely visiting the spot, transients among the thin posts that stood unmoving, as if for all time.

venice, italy

Bagnoreggio

The village of Bagnoreggio, one of the oldest hilltop villages in Italy, begs the questions, "why?" and "How?"

The first might be easier to answer. One can imagine that living in an earthen fortress would have the same advantages as a man-made one. Is there anywhere or anything you could not see from atop that pinnacle?

The question of "how" is a bit trickier. How was such a village, in such a remote location, successfully built? Perhaps the answer is better left to historians or tour guides.

There is, however, one reply that every viewer with a grand aesthetic sense might offer the village of Bagnoreggio: Thank you.

umbria, italy

Ristorante Puny

In the tiny fishing village of Portofino, an Italian chef has made a big name for himself.

Heads of state, traveling dignitaries and distinguished tourists — and apparently at least one motorcyclist — have graced the chef's namesake, Ristorante Puny.

The day of our visit, we were unable to partake of the restaurant's culinary treasures, but we felt fortunate to enjoy its visual offerings: pristine white linens, golden oak chairs, and rich green canopies of vegetation and fabric, all set against a terra cotta backdrop — all waiting for Chef Puny to make an appearance in the midst of his assiduous lunchtime preparations.

portofino, italy

Italian Riviera

Things are not always as they appear. Then again, that's the magic of photography.

On first glance, the village of Portofino seems to be floating on the sea, like a large cruise ship. In reality, its buildings are securely grounded on land and its enterprises securely rooted in traditional fishing.

The green hills and bright sky suggest a warm season and warm air. The day we photographed the area, however, snow remained on the hills and a chill remained in the air.

The calm water implies peace and quiet. In actuality, as we shot the picturesque scene, we were startled by the sudden roaring of not one but eight Apache helicopters.

portofino, italy

Amalfi Coast

South of the Bay of Naples on the Amalfi coast, lies a perfect little village — otherwise known as Positano.

In our mind's eye, we see Positano's creation. A lone explorer spots the hillside, and is inexorably drawn, not by the beaches, which are neither expansive nor pristine, but by something inexplicable. Is it the dancing blue of the ocean? The dotted green of the cliff-side? Or is it, perhaps, some inward recognition of the kinship between man and his earth, between his challenges and those of the land? Hanging over the sea, clinging to the rough terrain, digging in wherever the least bit of welcome soil will allow. In the perfect little village of Positano, we find ourselves wondering, is tenacity the father of perfection?

Amalfi coast, Italy

Now is the Magic Light

You never know what you might miss if you're looking only for the obvious. Camogli, Italy, is one of those places. On the other side of the peninsula from the more popular Portofino, clusters of unassuming, amber buildings rise from the water like patches of golden sunflowers from a green field. You might never notice them if you haven't seen them in the glory of a perfect sunset, when their simple faces take on a blushing radiance. From across the harbor, I knew what I was waiting for. So did the amiable Italian gentleman whose terrace had witnessed this scene before. Time passed, an hour, more; I could see the light changing, I could see it coming, painting new color on the village and the water and the villas climbing up the mountain behind them, the pine trees hanging over the cliffs. As I began shooting, the two of us exchanged glances, and he spoke. "Now is the magic light."

camogli, italy

Poo-Pah

We happened upon an unlikely tourist in the Italian village of Bellagio. As we rounded a corner in this beautiful town on Lake Como, we interrupted a small visitor enjoying the sights from his perch atop stone steps: a small, yellow dog. His coat was the same hue as the walls around him that framed the view to the lake below. He, like us, had strayed from Bellagio's heart, a bustling center of hotels, restaurants, cafes and shops. And "Poo-Pah," like us, spent a serene moment lost in that quiet, colorful alleyway.

Bellagio, Italy

The Guardian

I had waked past a courtyard several times on my way to and from my hotel in Ravello, Italy. The scene kept catching my eye, but the timing never seemed right for a shot — until the day I walked past and saw something waiting for his time, as well. A gray cat hung to the thick, gnarly vine that climbed one of the walls in this interior courtyard. Not wanting to disturb him in his mission, I walked past the entrance out of his view, and set up my camera with my 300-mm lens. Then I stole back to the doorway, lying in wait much as he was, each for our respective "prey." I got in three shots, before whatever had caught his eye evaded him or lost his interest. He jumped down, and the hunt was over, for both of us.

Ravello, Italy

High Ground

If you can't see where a path leads, do you still follow it?

We came upon a path meandering through the Dolomites in Italy. Others had obviously followed it, as it was well worn. But how far it went, and where, we could not tell.

In the end, we found it more intriguing to speculate than to ascertain. To allow our minds if not our feet to explore the path as it ascended inexorably to a place unknown but most certainly higher than where we began.

Dolomites, Italy

Room with a View

The "bluest view in the world" hangs from a cliff on Italy's Amalfi coast. It is called Ravello. South of Naples, between Sorento to the north and Salerno to the south, the otherwise quiet village of Ravello, practically shouts a blue magnificence. From its perch on the backbone of a mountain, Ravello calls out to its neighbors, the coastlines, as they spill open to the cerulean wonders of the Mediterranean. Standing at the edge of the sea, as we did, at the ancient Hotel Palazzo Sasso, a visitor immediately understands the appellation "bluest view;" azure sky meets sapphire sea and there seems no other color in the world but blue.

Ravello, Italy

The Grace of Light

In a little glen near Montalcino, the church St. Antimo stands gracefully among equally artful wild flowers, cyprus trees, and olive trees. Inside this beautiful church, light streams through arching windows as it has for more than 900 years. The abbey that was once its neighbor and its elder by more than 300 years, has vanished save for its foundation. Yet sunlight seems to have taken up permanent residence in the church, warming the coolest of stone, illuminating the mosaic of marble on floors and walls, and bending to the ancient carving of sturdy columns — gently touching all, like grace itself.

Tuscany, Italy

The Passage of Time

We saw time passing before us in more than one way in Cortona, a town in Tuscany. Outside a regal doorway, we waited, and waited some more, for the Tuscan sun to brighten the skies dulled by lingering thunderstorms. Then, almost without warning, the storms began to pass. Time suddenly became short. After hours of waiting, we found ourselves hurrying to get the shot before the light overpowered the scene and set up contrasts too stark for our purposes. Moments before the sun reappeared, a warm glow pervaded the air, evenly lighting an uneven scene. While stucco succumbed to the effects of time, crumbling from the walls, the door within stood fast. And our time vanished, fading into the image as the steps below the door disappeared into the time-worn stone of the street.

Tuscany, Italy

Nordic Light

About 250 miles north of the Arctic Circle (and a four-hour boat ride from anywhere), lies an island chain off the coast of Norway that must be seen to be believed. Views are dramatic and villages are quiet. Mountainous terrain serves as the often startling backdrop in a land where fishing is the industry of survival. The last day we were to be in this area, we got up at 5 a.m., hoping to avail ourselves of the particularly interesting light of the early morning. By the time we discovered the fishing village of Hamnoy — about an hour later — the sun's rays were just peeking through the low clouds. Fickle as it was, the sun cooperated just long enough for us to get several shots. Oranges, golds, reds — all revealed themselves brilliantly, dramatically, shining in stark contrast against the jagged mountains towering in the background, dark and ominous.

Hamnoy, Norway

Greystoke

Near the Lake District of northern England, we found a perfect window to the world in a town called Greystoke.

With clouds reflecting back at us, that window — owned by an accomplished mountain climber (and gardener, apparently) — showed us an image with the substance, balance and light we cherish, and continually seek.

Lake District, England

Green Shutters

If ever time was of the essence, it was when we set up to photograph a pair of shutters on a house in the Italian Alps near Lake Idro. For one fleeting moment, the light was perfect, the scene was perfect, the colors were perfect. We clicked the shutter. The next moment, a torrential rain came down and the perfect scene was washed away.

Italian Alps

Shady Cat

photographers often avoid exposures with full sun, as intense lighting is seldom conductive to establishing visual depth.

In the bright Mediterranean, the midday sun can literally drive a photographer indoors — unless there's a compelling reason to make an exception. we found one such exception, in the colors and shapes on a terrace in santorini, atypically enhanced and dramatically delineated by the bold light. The light even made a subject of another creature hesitant to leave: a cat whose dark shape joined itself with the deep shadows on the wall.

santorini, greece

A Bouquet of Color

Have you ever felt that something good is waiting right around the corner, but you can't seem to get there?

During several trips to Alsace, France, a little street kept attracting our attention. But each time, something was amiss. Scaffolding cluttered walls, paint colors waged war with themselves, light failed to cooperate with its subjects.

One more trip, one more try, and we finally rounded that street's "corner." Peaceful colors, tidy surroundings, and willing light all came together. And the alleyway's hinted potential burst forth like the blooms and foliage running down the bricks and pouring through the shutters.

Alsace, France

Etched Memories

Human history, even as rich as it is, can still only provide the barest traces of the innumerable people who have passed through this world. A notable few are remembered here and there; the famous and infamous find their way into the history books.

But what of the others, seemingly less significant, those of whom we'll never learn? Where are they memorialized?

In a church in Heilgenblut, Austria, we found evidence that at least a few have taken it upon themselves to be remembered in some fashion. Timeworn pews, aglow with light streaming through the church's gothic windows, are etched with the names of many who visited there. But the question remains: As they gazed at the cross at the far end of the room, who were they hoping would not forget them?

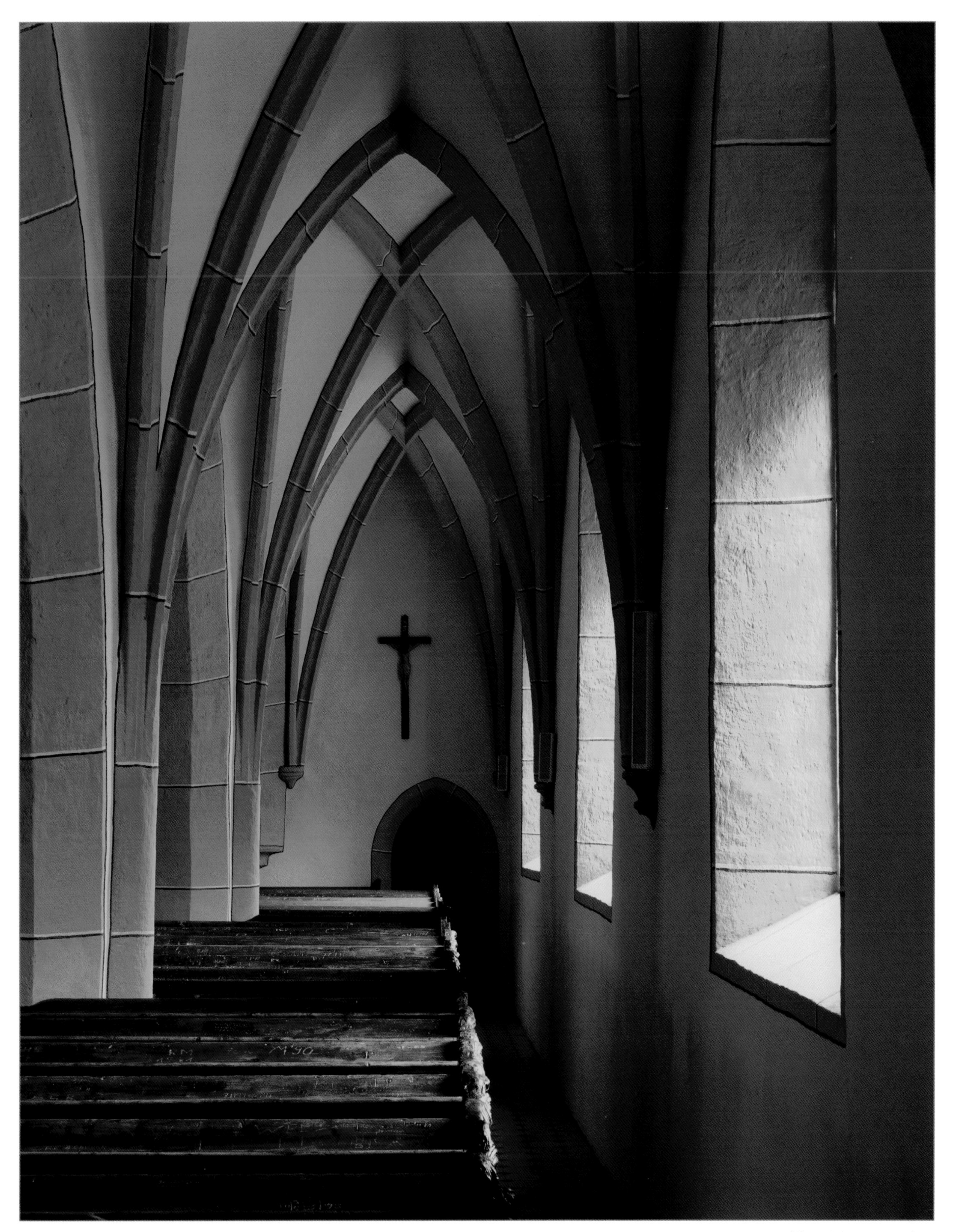

Heiligenblut, Austria

After the Rain

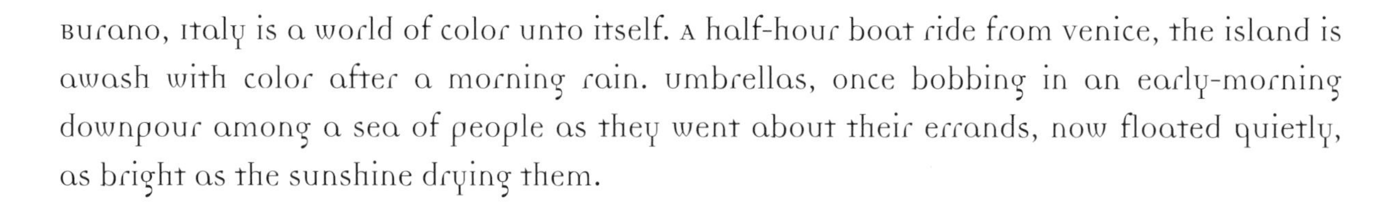

Burano, Italy is a world of color unto itself. A half-hour boat ride from Venice, the island is awash with color after a morning rain. Umbrellas, once bobbing in an early-morning downpour among a sea of people as they went about their errands, now floated quietly, as bright as the sunshine drying them.

Burano, Italy

Alley Cats

we returned to a colorful alley we discovered yesterday, when the light was less than ideal and bicycles dominated the shot we wanted.

we found, in their place, two cats that showed every intention of remaining — even if elusive subjects — and thus became the very life of the shot.

Alsace, France

Ascension

A retrospective look at a set of stairs in Dubrovnik, Yugoslavia, seems much the same as our initial impression. The perspectives are different, but the implications are similar.

Then, as now, our viewpoint is limited. When we took the shot, we were unaware of the impending war that would break out between the Serbs and the Croats just two years later. Today, unable to return to the troubled region, we are unaware of the fate of those steps.

The stairs themselves echo life's journey and its varying perspectives. Like life, they are full of "pits," yet they always seem to lead upward. Another, unseen step awaits the last, each a plateau broad and sturdy enough to provide support until the next step is taken. Seldom existing independently, they serve as a path, a way of access, to something beyond. If we could pan out from the scene and get the whole perspective, we might see a glimpse of what rests at the top. And, if we could return, we might see the way unfortunately blocked. Instead, we are thankful that our lasting — albeit limited — impression is of ascension.

dubrovnik, croatia

Capri

When you see the opportunity to get a bird's eye view of life, take it.

Granted, you might have to stand on the edge of a cliff to get this lofty perspective — as is the case on the island of Capri — but it's worth any trepidation you might feel perched on a ledge 300 feet above the ocean. From Capri, which lies just outside the Bay of Naples, both Naples and Mount Vesuvius are visible in the distance. The island itself is lush with vegetation. The ocean is Mediterranean-blue and crystal-clear to the bottom, even to the point where a boat floating atop it can see its own shadow in the depths of the water. From the cliffs of Capri, as perhaps in life, one can see the depth and width and height of at least one small, but grand, world.

capri, italy

Crossroads

As we were traveling through the quaint town of Ballyvaughn, we came upon a man selling photographs of a dog sitting on his donkey for 50 pence. We offered this very chatty, kind old character a pound to omit the dog and the donkey from the scene and allow us to take a shot of him.

He agreed, and we came away with an image of a memorable scene that could be found on any street in Ireland — a jumble of signs leading the way around the countryside, with Lisdoonvarna in both directions!

county clare, ireland

De Barra

The only sign missing from the front window of a pub in Clonakilty was one reading, "Come on in."

But from the looks of it, no such invitation was necessary. An eclectic collection of fliers, posters, cards and other printed mementos did the trick.

In getting close enough to read the signs, you'd also invariably catch sight of the activity on the other side of the windows. Curiosity would draw you in the door, and the allure of a pint might keep you there.

county cork, ireland

Lofoten Wall

This village is simply one of the prettiest in Norway. These massive, jagged peaks tower over the fishing village protecting the many inland-fishing lanes from the North Sea. This isn't the easiest place to reach in Norway, but then if everyone had access to it, this village would lose its unspoiled charm. It's fantastic the way the local people embrace their heritage and enjoy their simple livelihood of fishing, crafts and dancing to the polka played on traditional accordions.

Reine, Norway

Oberammergau Door

Trouble can be a blessing in disguise.

In a very crowded Oberammergau, congested by throngs of visitors come to see the Passion Play, we were struggling to find a parking place when we happened upon a treasure in fresco.

"The human being lives only a short while. All the world, with all its beauty, will pass away. It is only One who will stay eternally, and we are in His hands."

True enough, and yet how lucky we are to have chanced upon this testament before it, too, passed away.

oberammergau, germany

San Giovanni

There's something reassuring about knowing your place.

The San Giovanni church doesn't compete with its surroundings. It is perfectly content to be what it is. In the midst of a massive valley and the towering Dolomite peaks, it is a pretty little church, decorated with delicate scroll-work, a painting of San Giovanni, a useful steeple — and three pews.

St. Magdalena, Italy

A Wave of Color

Kinsale, Ireland, on the southern Cork coast, is a generally active village. Fishing occupies the time and interests of many. Good restaurants abound. Bread-and-breakfasts line the colorful streets.

But even in this lively village, one street in particular stood out. It just couldn't stay still!

Colors - bold purples, excited yellows, and flashy reds — seemed to jump from the walls of the buildings. Flowers burst from windows, sills and containers. Even the sidewalks undulated — as they had been constructed with dips and rises to escort rain waters away from doorways. And the result? A veritable wave of color.

county cork, ireland

Whispering Winds

A photograph captures a single moment, briefly halting both time and movement. But in the Black Valley of Ireland's County Kerry, neither time nor movement could be contained by a still image.

As a swirling wind pressed through the valley, tufts of stiff grass swayed and rustled, murmuring to one another. Leaves atop an old tree blurred with the breeze, leaving an impression on film as ghostly as the house it shrouded — a domain perhaps once lively but abandoned when its residents succumbed to the pressures of famine.

As we looked down a road winding to the ancient house, we couldn't help wondering if the wind were not the only voice still whispering in those hills.

county kerry, ireland

Still Waters

we see more clearly in still waters.

when life seems to rage around us, our vision can become clouded. But when we stop to rest, the waters stop churning. we turn to our thoughts, and we find a crystal quietness, crisp as a shining white boat, cutting the glassiness of a Norwegian mountain lake. In its perfect reflection, we remember that we are not truly alone, but embraced by solitary tranquility.

Lofoten Islands, Norway

from the field

Deb looking for angles while Haley reads.
KINSALE, IRELAND

The shepherd's daughter and Grandma tending the flock.
CORTINA, ITALY

A happy lass in Ireland.
COUNTY KERRY, IRELAND

Haley standing in front of image "Sea of Blue."
KINSALE, IRELAND

Waiting for the light. Deb shooting in the Black Valley.
COUNTY KERRY, IRELAND

Haley poses with Scottish boys on a special occasion.
ABERDEEN, SCOTLAND

John, looking much younger, with Cucciolo, which is Italian for "puppy."
ITALIAN RIVIERA

John and Deb hiking in the Dolomites.
NEAR CORTINA, ITALY

Scruffy dog guarding scruffy hardware store.
MYKONOS, GREECE

An elderly Greek woman outside her home.
SANTORINI, GREECE

Haley feeding the pigeons in St. Mark's Square.
VENICE, ITALY

John shooting the rocky coast of the Bere Peninsula.
IRELAND

from the field

John and Haley enjoying the sunshine on the beach.

COUNTY GALWAY, IRELAND

John and Haley investigating an old abandoned farmhouse in the Black Valley.

COUNTY KERRY, IRELAND

Haley feeding orphaned lambs.

COUNTY KERRY, IRELAND

Haley holding a Border Collie pup outside a small Irish home belonging to a kind elderly irishman.

COUNTY KERRY, IRELAND

Deb and Haley at the Cliffs of Moher.

COUNTY CLARE, IRELAND

Haley lounging in a colorful doorway.

ROTHENBURG, GERMANY

Haley kissing the Blarney Stone.

BLARNEY CASTLE, IRELAND

Deb and Haley by a beautiful roadside shrine. This was one of many that we saw in this region.

BERCHTESGADEN, GERMANY

Irish gentlemen enjoying an afternoon pint (or two).

CLONAKILTY, IRELAND

Haley standing next to a bagpiper playing an eerie tune just outside the dungeon of Dunnottar Castle. William Wallace once fought here.

NEAR STONEHAVEN, SCOTLAND

John shooting in one of our favorite villages.

ALSACE, FRANCE

194

Index

Austria

Etched Memories 166
Swan Lake 32

Croatia

Ascension 172

Czech Republic

Charles Bridge 28
Embracing the Night 24
Reflections of Prague 26

England

Bicycle 112
Cambray's Farmhouse 98
Castle Combe 100
Castle Gardens 108
Gatekeeper 110
Gold Hill 102
Greystoke 158
Rose Cottage 104
Tranquil Reflections 106
Veiled Garden 80

France

A Bouquet of Color 164
Alley Cats 170
Bon Appétit 62
Brushstrokes 70
Corner Stones 52

France (cont.)

Floral Ascent 58
La Maison Antoinette 82
Les Fleurs a Suzette 74
Marie's Hamlet 84
Menu of the Day 78
Monet's Inspiration 76
Poulbot 72
Provence in Bloom 54
Roman Numerals 64
Rue-du-Fleuri 56
Steps in Time 66
Vintage Fox 68

Germany

Alpine Church 22
Oberammergau Door 182

Greece

A Day's Repose 20
Caldera 30
Mykonos 40
Rising Light 18
Shady Cat 162

Ireland

A Resting Place 12
A Soft Day 92
A Wave of Color 186
Celtic Passage 90
Cottage Thatch 86

Ireland (cont.)

Crossroads 176
De Barra 178
Dusk 88
O'Shea's 96
Sea of Blue 94
St. Finbar's Retreat 8
Whispering Winds 188

Italy

A Walk to Remember 46
After the Rain 168
Amalfi Coast 140
Awakening 44
Bagnoreggio 134
Burano 120
Café Arcade 130
Capri 174
Cucciolo 114
First Mate 116
Green Shutters 160
High Ground 148
Italian Riviera 138
Now is the Magic Light ...142
Orvieto 126
Poo-Pah 144
Ristorante Puny 136
Rocky Cathedrals 10
Room with a View 150
San Giovanni 184
Sangiovese 128
Scattered Blossoms 38

Italy (cont.)

Sunlit Gondolier 6
Table for Two 122
The Grace of Light 152
The Guardian 146
The Journey 14
The Passage of Time 154
Three Pear 124
Time in a Bottle 60
Venetian Dance 132
Vernazza 48
Wash Day 118

Norway

Lofoten Wall 180
Nordic Harbour 42
Nordic Light 156
Still Waters 190

Portugal

Life is but a Dream 36

Scotland

Eilean Donan 16
Old Course 50

Switzerland

Fallen Petals 34